LIFE
SKILL
HANDBO

MW00812015

# Everyday *Household* *Tasks*

Grocery Shopping | Cooking
Caring for Clothes | Home Maintenance and Decorating

# LIFE SKILLS

## H A N D B O O K S

Car and Driver

Community Resources and Safety

Consumer Spending

Everyday Household Tasks

Getting Ahead at Work

Health and Wellness

Managing Money

Moving Out on Your Own

Transportation

Workplace Readiness

SADDLEBACK
EDUCATIONAL PUBLISHING
www.sdlback.com

ISBN: 978-1-68021-984-5
eBook: 978-1-64598-782-6

Printed in Malaysia
26 25 24 23 22    1 2 3 4 5

# TABLE OF CONTENTS

# Grocery Shopping

Smart grocery shoppers have a plan. They know exactly what they have at home and what they need from the store. The best shoppers also know how to buy **nutritious**, high-quality food *and* save money. What could you do to eat better and spend less on groceries?

## New Habits for a New Year

Most years, Kevin didn't think about making New Year's resolutions. But this year, he had a definite goal in mind. He wanted to get better at buying groceries.

Kevin's friend thought he was being silly. "Who cares about buying groceries?" she asked.

"I do," Kevin said. "For two main reasons."

One reason was cost. Kevin knew he spent a lot of money at the grocery store. After all, he went there three or four times a week. He usually stopped on his way home from work. Yet it felt like he never had anything in the house to eat. Kevin always had food. But none of it seemed to go together to make a meal.

As a result, Kevin often ended up eating random foods. One night for dinner, he had a frozen burrito and a can of peaches. Sometimes, he didn't bother trying to figure out what to eat. He'd just order a pizza.

Kevin's second concern was health. His diet wasn't healthy. He rarely bought fresh fruits and vegetables. It took time to clean and cook them. Plus, they spoiled if he didn't eat them right away.

Instead, Kevin ate a lot of **ready-made** foods. These were canned, boxed, and frozen products. He liked how easy these foods were to prepare. Most of them, he just popped into the microwave. But he knew these foods weren't very good for him.

Kevin resolved to change his eating and shopping **habits**. He rarely thought about his meals in advance. That meant he made many trips to the grocery store. Learning to shop smarter would save him time and money. It would also help him improve his health.

# Chapter 1

## Buying Grocery Staples

Grocery **staples** are the basic food items you use again and again. They are foods you need on hand to put together meals on a regular basis.

Think about your favorite meals. What foods, spices, and other items do you need to make them? These are called **ingredients**. If any will stay fresh in your refrigerator, freezer, or **pantry**, consider stocking up. These staples will make putting together a dish quick and easy.

### Common Grocery Staples

Many grocery staples are nonperishable. That means they can be stored for a long time without going bad. Not all staples can be left in the pantry though. Frozen foods should stay frozen until you're ready to use them. Just remember to plan enough time for them to thaw before you need them for a meal. Some staples, like eggs and butter, need to be kept in the refrigerator. Here are other common grocery staples:

- canned or dried beans
- pasta
- jarred sauces
- frozen produce
- frozen meat
- rice
- nut butters

- coffee and tea
- cereal
- crackers
- honey
- oatmeal
- popcorn

- potatoes
- canned tuna or chicken
- condiments

## Other Staples to Have on Hand

Do you bake often? If so, staples for your kitchen should include baking supplies. These are items such as flour, sugar, and salt. Baking powder, baking soda, and yeast are also good to have.

Herbs and spices are other staples. Rosemary and oregano add flavor to food. Cinnamon and pepper do too.

What about **condiments**? Products such as soy sauce, ketchup, mustard, mayonnaise, and barbecue sauce are staples.

## Shopping for Staples

When you shop, always be aware of how long a product will stay fresh. Fresh fruits and vegetables can't be stored for very long. Frozen fruits and vegetables can be stored in the freezer for months. Canned products can last for years.

Stock your pantry with canned goods. Fill your freezer with frozen foods. But buy only as much fresh food as you can eat in a few days.

## Storing Foods

Certain foods should be stored in the refrigerator or freezer. For example, dairy products must be refrigerated. These include items such as milk and cheese.

Many canned and bottled foods must be refrigerated after they've been opened. Otherwise, they will spoil. Look for this requirement on food labels.

Certain fresh fruits and vegetables can be stored in the refrigerator. Grains, such as breads and muffins, can be too. Some, but not all, of these foods need to be kept cold. Many are fine stored on a countertop or in the pantry. However, keeping them cool may help them last longer.

Other foods should be stored in your pantry. Foods stored in a pantry are often called dry goods and canned goods.

For all kinds of foods, pay attention to the expiration date. Many foods can still be eaten past this date. The quality and taste just won't be as good. However, some expired foods could make you very sick. These include many types of meat, seafood, soft cheeses, and some fruits and vegetables.

### The Facts About Expiration Dates

Here's a surprising fact: Food isn't usually spoiled or harmful after its expiration date. It just won't taste as good. The quality may not be as good either.

Some grocery stores remove products from shelves after their expiration dates. But they don't need to. You should check products' expiration dates while you shop. Then you won't buy something that is about to expire. Look for these codes and know what they mean:

- **Sell by:** This is the date that a product should be sold by. After this date, stores should remove the product from shelves. Food is still safe to eat after this date.

- **Best by:** The flavor or quality may not be as good after this date. But the food can still be eaten.

- **Use by:** This is the last day the food's manufacturer stands by its quality.

## Setting Up Your Pantry

The goods in your pantry should be organized in a **logical** way. For example, keep pasta and pasta sauces next to each other. You might also group similar items. Cereals may all go in one place. Baking ingredients might be kept together.

Figure out your own pantry plan. Then stick with it. That will make it easier to find things.

# Chapter 2

## Reading Grocery Ads

Lissa has been looking at grocery store advertisements. These are also called ads. Sometimes she goes online to view store ads. She also looks through the newspaper for **coupons**. These help her save money on certain products.

In the local newspaper this morning, Lissa saw two ads. She looked at them closely to see which store had the better deals for items on her shopping list. Lissa knows that comparison shopping will help her find the best bargains.

## Learn What Experienced Shoppers Know

Lissa decided to go to Smart Mart to do her grocery shopping. She liked the price on the blue cheese salad dressing. She'd never seen it so low. Her mother called this kind of low-priced item a "loss leader." The store sold the product at a loss just to get customers to come in.

When Lissa entered the store, she saw a display of canned tuna. On top was a sign. It said, "Brand X Tuna 99¢."

This special hadn't been in the morning newspaper ad. Maybe the store had gotten a good buy on the tuna. Now it wanted to pass the savings on to its customers. This seemed like a bargain. Lissa put six cans into her cart. Then she continued shopping.

Later, Lissa turned down the aisle where tuna was regularly sold. She noticed that Brand Y was selling for $0.89. Lissa compared the two brands of tuna side by side. Both were chunk light tuna and packed in water. They were also the same weight. Brand Y was the better deal.

Lissa put six cans of Brand Y tuna into her cart. She put the Brand X tuna back where she'd found it.

## Where to Find Grocery Store Coupons

- **Sunday newspaper:** Cut out coupons from grocery store ads.

- **Weekly mailers:** Some stores send flyers each week containing sale information and coupons.

- **Internet:** Do a search for coupon websites, and print out coupons or save them to your cell phone's digital wallet or an app. You may also find coupon codes that can be used when shopping for groceries online.

- **Manufacturers' websites:** If you have favorite products, check the manufacturers' websites for coupons. Sign up for their email list and receive product information and coupons in your inbox. You can also check their social media pages for special offers.

- **Food packages:** Look on the backs and insides of packages. Coupons are sometimes printed there.

- **Customer service desk:** Ask for coupon books and store coupons. Some may also be found on store websites.

- **Store apps:** Check to see if your favorite stores have their own apps. You might be able to find coupons there. The companies that make your favorite products may also have apps that offer savings.

This made Lissa think of something else her mother had told her. A "special" may or may not be a good deal. A sign that says the price is $0.99 "today only" suggests the price will be higher tomorrow. But the price might actually be lower tomorrow. There is no way to tell. Careful shoppers always compare prices, no matter what a sign says.

When Lissa got to the yogurt display, she saw a sign. It said, "10 for $5." Lissa put five containers in her cart. She knew she didn't have to buy ten. These items were $0.50 each, no matter how many she bought. Stores want people to buy a lot. But it is better to buy only what you need.

Lissa remembered she had a coupon for another brand of yogurt. She decided not to use it though. It required buying ten containers. That was more than she wanted.

---

**How Do Coupons Work?**

Coupons are like money. You give them to the cashier when you pay for your groceries. The value of each coupon is subtracted from what you owe.

In most cases, coupons can be used only to buy specific products. For instance, a coupon for laundry detergent will be good only for a particular brand. Often, coupons also require buying a particular size or number of items.

Coupons have expiration dates too. Most stores won't take coupons past these dates. Some stores will though. Be sure to ask about the store's policy.

## Tips for Shopping With Coupons

- Collect coupons only for items you normally buy.

- Don't use coupons to buy name-brand items that cost more than store-brand items.

- Find out if your store has certain days when it doubles the value of coupons.

- Don't use coupons that require you to buy more of something than you'll use.

- Use an app or your digital wallet to collect digital coupons.

- Organize paper coupons by category in an envelope or file.

- Once a month, go through your coupons. Throw out any that have expired.

- Have the coupons you plan to use ready before you get to the checkout to pay for your groceries.

- Make sure the cashier rings up coupon items correctly.

# Chapter 3

## Planning Meals

Do you plan your meals ahead of time? Whether cooking for your family or just for yourself, planning is key. It makes shopping and cooking easier.

## Making a Plan

Meal planning will help you save time and money. It can also help you eat healthy.

Set aside time each week to make your plan. Create a weekly calendar using a computer or app. You can also make one on paper. Plan what you'll eat each day for every meal. Think about ways you can use ingredients in more than one dish. This will stretch your food budget. Less food will be wasted too.

When planning, think about what ingredients you already have. These might be staples. They may also be things you need to use up before they go bad. Try to work these ingredients into your meals. Next, make a shopping list for ingredients you need to buy. Stick to this list at the store. That way, you'll only buy food you plan to eat.

## Reading Nutrition Labels

Packaged foods have nutrition labels. Learn to read them to determine three things:

1. **What's the serving size?** Check how much is considered one serving. For example, a serving may be ¼ cup. The other information on the label is based on that serving size.

2. **What's in it?** Review the nutritional information. Vitamins, calcium, and fiber contribute to good health. Too much saturated (solid) fat and sodium (salt) can be harmful to the body.

3. **Is it right for you?** People have different dietary needs and preferences. Use what you read on labels to decide if a food is a good choice for you.

# Nutrition Facts

Serving Size 1/4 Cup (30g)
Servings Per Container About 8

**Amount Per Serving**

**Calories** 200    Calories from Fat 150

|  | % Daily Value* |
|---|---|
| **Total Fat** 17g | **26**% |
| Saturated Fat 2.5g | **13**% |
| Trans Fat 0g | |
| **Cholesterol** 0mg | **0**% |
| **Sodium** 120mg | **5**% |
| **Total Carbohydrate** 7g | **2**% |
| Dietary Fiber 2g | **8**% |
| Sugars 1g | |
| **Protein** 5g | |

| Vitamin A 0% | • | Vitamin C 0% |
|---|---|---|
| Calcium 4% | • | Iron 8% |

*Percent Daily Values are based on a 2,000 calorie diet.

## Variety

Many people who meal plan will make big **batches** of food. Then they'll eat the same meal several times throughout the week. This takes some of the thinking out of getting meals on the table. You can make a big pot of soup on Sunday. Then on Monday, Wednesday, and Friday, you can plan to eat soup for lunch.

Still, we all like a little variety in our meals. It's no fun to eat the same thing every day. Smart meal planners think of different foods they enjoy. Then they rotate these throughout their meal plan. Having a go-to list of these dishes makes meal planning simple.

## Reading About Ingredients

The labels on packaged foods include a list of ingredients. These are listed in order from largest to smallest amount. Learn to read these labels and determine what they mean. Here are some common ingredients to look for:

- **Whole grains:** Products with terms like "whole grain" and "multigrain" in their names may not mean they are truly "whole grain." To find out, see whether a whole grain (not just wheat or flour) comes first in the list of ingredients.

- **Sugars:** Some sugars are found naturally in certain foods. Others are added. Check the label to see how much added sugar is in a product.

- **Sodium (salt):** A small quantity can still be a lot. Look for a very low percentage. Also look for products labeled "low sodium."

- **Good fats:** Oils are fats that are liquid at room temperature. Most are good for you. These come from vegetables, seeds, and nuts.

- **Bad fats:** Solid fats, which come from animal products, are usually bad for you. They include butter, cream, lard, and fat from meat. Other bad fats are found in stick margarine and a few oils.

# Chapter 4

## Getting the Best Value

Most people don't like to waste things, especially money. But saving money doesn't come naturally to everyone.

Luckily, you can learn how to be a smart grocery shopper. For instance, wise shoppers know what to buy at different kinds of stores. These may be discount stores or warehouse clubs. They may also be supermarkets or farmers markets.

## How to Get the Most for Your Money

Follow these tips to get the best value for your money:

1. **Make a grocery list.** Write down the ingredients you need for a recipe. When you shop, keep your options open. For example, do you need to buy Red Delicious apples or will another kind work? See what's on sale. Also keep variety in mind. If you've written down "salad stuff," don't always get the same ingredients. Maybe a different kind of lettuce is cheaper. Try to buy locally

grown **produce** when you can. These foods are fresher and more nutritious.

2. **Don't shop when you're hungry.** You'll be more likely to buy food you don't need. You're also more likely to buy ready-made foods. These usually aren't the best value.

3. **Use coupons.** When you shop, bring only the coupons you know you're going to need. Don't buy things you don't need just to save a few cents.

4. **Don't go down every aisle.** In most supermarkets, fresh foods are placed around the edges of the store. They line the sides and the back. The middle aisles are filled with ready-made foods, snacks, and other items. Shop with a list. Avoid going down unnecessary aisles.

### Fresh Produce All Year

If you live in an area with cold winters, you can't buy locally grown produce all year long. But thanks to refrigerated shipping, you can buy your favorite fruits and vegetables even in winter. This produce comes from countries near Earth's equator. These places are always warm. Produce also comes from places far south of the equator. The seasons there are opposite those in North America.

About 50% of vegetables imported by the United States come from Mexico. Mexico also grows 40% of our imported fruits.

5. **Look at the top and bottom shelves.** That's where you'll usually find the best bargains. Why? The average supermarket shopper is a woman about 5'4" tall. Stores often display the most expensive products at her eye level.

6. **Read and compare labels.** Study the list of ingredients to see what you're getting for your money. Don't be fooled by fancy product names and package designs. Two products may look very different. One may be more expensive. But the ingredients may be all the same.

7. **Don't always buy name-brand products.** There's a reason the name brands cost more than the store brands. That reason is advertising. It costs a lot of money to advertise products on TV. Store-brand products are usually just as good. But they cost much less.

8. **Shop for seasonal foods.** If you buy produce that's out of season where you live, it will cost more. That's because it had to be shipped from far away. A quick online search can help you figure out what's in season in your area. Save even more money by growing your own seasonal produce. You may also consider signing up for a CSA program. CSA stands for community-supported agriculture. People who join a CSA pay money to support local farmers. In return, the farmers supply CSA members with fresh, locally grown produce throughout the growing season.

9. **Figure out the unit price.** Knowing the unit price lets you compare the costs of different products in equal amounts. For example, suppose you see two bottles of juice. One is $3.49.

The other is $2.69. Don't assume that the lower-priced bottle is the best buy. It might contain half the amount of juice as the other bottle. To get the best value, figure out the cost per unit. Sometimes, the unit price is provided with the product information on the shelf at the store. If not, figure out the unit price for yourself. To do this, divide the price by the number of units.

# Where to Buy Groceries

Many different places sell groceries. Prices can vary widely, depending on the location, size, and purpose of the store.

- **Markets are small stores that are often unique.** Some sell certain kinds of foods, such as ethnic foods. At some markets, you can find great deals on fresh produce.

- **Convenience stores sell grocery staples and snack foods.** They also offer a variety of other items. However, the selection is limited. Prices are higher too.

- **Grocery stores are often found in small communities.** Many are locally owned. They have a full selection of foods plus some household items. Prices are usually higher than at larger stores. But coupons are often offered in local newspapers and mailers.

- **Supermarkets are chains of big grocery stores that operate throughout a region.** Because of their large size, supermarkets usually have lower prices than other stores. They also tend to advertise a lot and provide coupons.

- **Discount stores and warehouse stores sell many things in addition to groceries.** All of their products tend to be sold at lower prices than found elsewhere. Warehouse stores usually require buying in large quantities. This is called buying in bulk. It's a great way to stock up and save on grocery staples. But don't buy more than you'll use before the products go bad.

- **Farmers markets are public gatherings of local farmers.** Fresh, local produce and products such as honey and cheese are sold there. Prices are often lower than in stores. Sometimes you can even bargain with sellers. At the end of the day, many farmers will sell their products at deep discounts. The more they sell, the less they have to pack up and take home.

- **Online grocery services are companies that partner with various stores.** Go online and fill a virtual shopping cart. For a small fee, someone will go to the store and do the actual shopping for you. Then they'll deliver the groceries right to your door. You can also choose to pick up your order at the store yourself. Someone will bring your groceries out to your car.

- **Meat and produce delivery services also send fresh food right to your home.** You can sign up to have your choice of meats delivered every few weeks or months. Fresh fruits and vegetables can be delivered too. Know that these subscription plans can be pricey. To save money, sign up for a service that delivers imperfect produce. These offer fruits and vegetables that don't look perfect but are still fine to eat.

- **Meal kits come with everything you need to make tasty meals at home.** You can sign up and pick your meals. Then fresh ingredients are shipped to your door. Everything you need, including the recipes, are all in the box. Some meal kits can be expensive.

# Cooking

Cooking shows make being in the kitchen look glamorous. But in real life, cooking involves preparing several meals a day—every day. To do that, you need to set up your kitchen with the right tools. You also need to know how to use a cookbook and follow a recipe. Having basic supplies and skills will help you be a good cook. It will also make your time in the kitchen more enjoyable.

# The Newest Cook in the Family

Maria grew up around food. Everyone in her family likes to cook. Because of this, they always have fantastic get-togethers. Maria looks forward to someday having them at her house.

Soon, Maria will have her first apartment. She will be done with nursing school next year. After that, she plans to move to the city. There, she will find a job.

Until then, Maria is living at home with her family. She likes helping her parents fix dinner. Her mom and dad appreciate her help. They are both busy with their jobs and their younger children's school and sports activities. Plus, Maria knows they sometimes get tired of having to put a meal on the table.

For her birthday, Maria received a cookbook from her grandmother. They made some of the recipes in it together. Working with her grandmother, Maria learned a lot about using a cookbook and following a recipe. Her grandmother had years of experience in the kitchen. She gave Maria great tips.

Maria has also started to collect items she will need for her own kitchen. Her parents have given her their old pots and pans. At a garage sale, Maria found mixing bowls and bakeware. These were in great shape. Plus, they only cost a few dollars.

It will take a while for Maria to get everything she needs. But that is okay. In the meantime, she is enjoying her role as the newest cook in the family.

# Chapter 1

## Setting Up a Kitchen

Are you ready to cook a meal? Make sure you have the right tools. A well-equipped kitchen has some basic equipment. You'll need a set of **utensils**, pots and pans, and bakeware. Storage products and **gadgets** are helpful too.

## Utensils

- mixing bowls of different sizes
- dry measuring cups
- clear-glass liquid measuring cup
- measuring spoons
- wooden spoons
- rubber spatulas
- flexible metal spatulas
- variety of knives
- sharpening steel for knives
- vegetable peeler
- long-handled fork
- long-handled spoon
- ladle
- slotted spoon
- tongs

- kitchen scissors
- pizza cutter
- bottle opener
- can opener
- grater and/or shredder
- small and large strainers
- colander
- kitchen timer
- cutting board
- rolling pin
- meat thermometer
- oven thermometer
- wire cooling rack
- vegetable steamer

### Cleaning Utensils: Wood Versus Plastic

Many kitchen utensils are made of wood or plastic. These materials need to be cleaned in different ways. Properly caring for your kitchen utensils will make them last longer.

**Wooden Utensils**

- Wash by hand with warm, soapy water. Rinse and pat dry with a clean towel. Then air-dry completely.

- Don't soak in water or put them in the dishwasher. Doing so will make the wood warp or crack.

- Protect against cracks using food-grade mineral oil. Pour a small amount of oil onto a cloth and rub it into the wood.

- Store in a clean, dry place.

**Plastic Utensils**

- Wash by hand or in the dishwasher.

- If necessary, soak in warm, soapy water. A nylon scrubbing pad may also be used. Don't use a metal pad. It will scratch.

- Wipe with vinegar to remove white spots (calcium deposits). Then rinse and dry. Don't use ammonia or bleach.

- Store in a clean, dry place.

## Pots and Pans

- 1-, 2-, and 3-quart covered saucepans
- 12- or 16-quart covered stockpot
- 4- or 6-quart covered Dutch oven
- 6- or 8-inch skillet
- 10-inch skillet
- 12-inch skillet
- wok
- roasting pan with rack
- pizza pan

### Buying a Basic Set of Knives

- **Chef's knife:** A chef's knife is long and wide. It's used for cutting, chopping, and slicing. Choose a knife with an 8- or 10-inch stainless steel blade. Keep the blade sharp by using a sharpening steel.

- **Slicing knife:** A slicing knife may also be called a carving knife. It has a long blade that is often 8 to 10 inches long. Slicing knives are used to cut cooked meat, fish, and poultry.

- **Paring knife:** A paring knife is similar to a chef's knife but smaller. The blade is usually 2 to 4 inches long. Paring knives are used for peeling and making other small cuts.

- **Serrated knife:** A serrated knife has small grooves in the blade and often a jagged edge. These features allow it to slice easily through bread and other soft foods without tearing them. Choose a serrated knife with a blade 6 to 8 inches long.

## Choosing a Stove: Gas or Electric?

Experienced cooks often have strong opinions about what type of stove they like. Some prefer to use a gas stove. Others like to cook on an electric stove. Here are a few of the advantages of both types.

**Gas stoves:**

- provide even heat. The amount of heat can also be changed immediately by turning the flame up or down.
- are usually less expensive to operate.
- can be used during a power outage.

**Electric stoves:**

- are easy to clean.
- present fewer fire hazards, as they don't have open flames.
- may often be easier and less expensive to install.

## Bakeware

- cookie sheets
- custard cups or ramekins
- muffin tins
- pie plates

- loaf pans
- baking dishes
- cake pans

## Food Storage Products

- containers/canisters
- foil
- clear plastic wrap
- wax paper

- parchment paper
- plastic bags (large and small)
- juice pitcher

## Useful Gadgets

- blender
- food processor
- coffeemaker
- juicer

- rice cooker
- toaster
- bread-making machine
- teakettle

## Getting What You Need

You don't have to buy all these items at once. Start with the ones that are most necessary for you. Go back through the lists. Think about how you'd use each item.

Remember, kitchen tools don't need to be brand-new. Many can be found at garage sales, estate sales, or secondhand stores. Buying used will save you money.

There are a few other items that might not be listed here. These are special tools or dishes you'll need to cook or bake your favorite recipes. As you spend more time in the kitchen, you'll learn what you need.

# Chapter 2

## Time-Savers

Claire takes classes in the morning. She has a part-time job in the afternoon. After work, she has to get dinner ready for her family.

But Claire doesn't get stressed about fixing dinner. Even though her time is limited, she knows she can do it.

Over the years, Claire has learned to plan ahead. She's also picked up some useful time-savers.

## Cooking in Bulk

On Saturday, Claire spends the afternoon cooking in **bulk**. First, she makes a big pot of spaghetti sauce. Next, she makes beef stew and a casserole. Claire divides everything into meal-size portions. These are then stored in the freezer.

At the end of the day, Claire has about 16 servings of spaghetti sauce. She has the same number of servings of stew and casserole.

Over the next few weeks, Claire can thaw what she needs for a meal. She can heat the frozen portions on the stove or in the microwave. This will save her a lot of time.

Cooking in bulk also saves cleanup time. Often, Claire has just one or two pots to clean.

## Ingredients to Have on Hand

Having a well-stocked pantry and freezer is important for any home cook. Some of the most useful ingredients to have on hand are canned and frozen vegetables.

These vegetables are cheaper than fresh produce. They're also easier to prepare. For example, a can of corn or green beans makes a quick and easy side dish. Frozen and canned vegetables are great additions to soups and stews too.

Canned and frozen vegetables don't have all of the nutritional benefits of fresh produce. But because they're so easy to prepare, you may serve vegetables more often.

## Using a Slow Cooker

Sometimes, Claire makes dinner using a slow cooker. This is an electric cooking pot. It cooks foods at low temperatures over a long period of time. One of Claire's favorite meals to make is chicken stew.

In the morning, Claire puts chicken, vegetables, and water in the pot. She adds a few spices for flavor. Then she turns on the cooker.

All day, the stew cooks slowly while Claire is at school and work. It's hot and ready to serve by dinnertime. The only cleanup is to wash out the pot.

## Using a Food Processor

Claire spends very little time chopping vegetables. She uses her food processor to chop, slice, grate, and mince them for her. In addition, the food processor mixes, grinds, and blends. It can even make dough for bread and pie.

## Using Nonstick Pots and Pans

Another time-saver is to use nonstick pots and pans. A special finish keeps food from sticking. This makes pots and pans much easier to clean. Use rubber or wooden utensils with this type of cookware. These won't scratch the nonstick coating.

## Using a Microwave

Claire's family likes baked potatoes. These need to cook for a long time though. In a regular oven, a large potato takes up to an hour to cook through.

To make baked potatoes in a hurry, Claire uses the microwave. This cuts down the cooking time by 40 minutes or more. Microwaved potatoes are a little different from those baked in a regular oven. Their skin doesn't get crispy. But Claire's family doesn't mind.

On busy days, Claire also uses the microwave to cook vegetables. She puts cut-up vegetables in a bowl and adds a little water. Then she covers the bowl and places it in the microwave. After cooking for about five minutes on high power, the vegetables are done. All Claire has to do is drain and season them.

Using the microwave saves both time and energy. Plus, cleanup is quick and easy.

## Microwave Safety Tips

- Remove all packaging before defrosting food in a microwave.

- Cook food immediately after defrosting it, especially meat.

- Don't let plastic wrap touch food that is being heated.

- Stir or turn food halfway through cooking. This allows it to cook evenly and all the way through.

- Don't use plastic storage containers to defrost or heat food. The plastic may melt or warp.

- Only use containers that are labeled "microwave safe."

- Don't use brown paper or plastic grocery bags, newspaper, plastic storage bags, or aluminum foil in a microwave. They may melt or catch fire.

- Never put metal containers or utensils in a microwave.

## Tips for Quick Cleanup

1. **Plan ahead.** Plan for the cleanup along with the meal. Something as simple as making room for leftovers in the refrigerator before the meal can save time later.

2. **Clean as you cook.** Fill the sink with warm, soapy water. Wash dishes and utensils as you use them. Soak large dishes in the sink to open up room in the dishwasher.

3. **Keep counters and other surfaces clean.** Wipe down counters after each use. This prevents messy buildup. Likewise, wipe up spills on the stove and in the microwave immediately after they happen.

4. **Use a scrap bowl.** Keep a bowl on your counter near the sink. Throw scraps into it as you clean and cut up vegetables, fruits, and other fresh ingredients. Empty the bowl into the trash after you've finished. You can also throw most food scraps into a composter, if you have one.

# Chapter 3

## Using a Cookbook

A good cookbook contains much more than recipes. It also has useful information about meal planning and cooking techniques. To find all this helpful information, you need to know how a cookbook is organized.

## How a Cookbook Is Organized

Like other books, most cookbooks have chapters. Cookbook chapters may be about different types of foods. Sometimes they are broken down into different types of meals, such as breakfast or special occasions.

Other chapters may be about certain topics. For instance, many cookbooks have chapters on food storage or where to find ingredients.

Finally, cookbooks usually have information that's helpful while you're cooking. This is often provided at the end of the book. There may be measurement charts and lists of ingredient substitutions.

Many cookbooks have a glossary too. This lists and defines cooking terms and techniques. There may also be an index. An index lists the ingredients, recipe names, tools, and more that are found throughout the cookbook. Page numbers are given so you can easily find what you're looking for.

# Review the Table of Contents

You can get a good overview of a cookbook by looking at its table of contents. Here's a sample:

## Table of Contents

## Go to Your Cookbook for Answers

Do you have a question about cooking? Use your cookbook to find the answer.

Suppose you ran out of sour cream but need it for a recipe. Look for a section on substitutions. Here you'll find information about what you can use instead. Maybe you're looking for a tasty snack to bring to a party. Check out any chapters that have recipes for appetizers or snacks.

Imagine a recipe says to char the meat. Do you know what that means? If not, you could look it up in the glossary.

Maybe you'd like some new ideas for ways to cook potatoes. You could find recipes and their page numbers by looking up "potatoes" in the index.

## Common Measurement Conversions

Do you know how many ounces are in a cup? What about how many cups are in a quart? To make sure you use the right amounts, look in your cookbook for a chart like this:

| This Amount | Equals This . . . | . . . and This |
|---|---|---|
| 1 teaspoon | $1/6$ fluid ounce | $1/3$ tablespoon |
| 1 tablespoon | $1/2$ fluid ounce | 3 teaspoons |
| $1/4$ cup | 2 fluid ounces | 4 tablespoons |
| $1/3$ cup | $2\ 2/3$ fluid ounces | $1/4$ cup + 4 teaspoons |
| $1/2$ cup | 4 fluid ounces | 8 tablespoons |
| 1 cup | 8 fluid ounces | $1/2$ pint |

## Online Tools

Another useful source of information about cooking is the internet. Websites offer everything from online cooking classes to information about special kitchen equipment.

Many websites offer lists of recipes. You can search them by name or by main ingredients. At many sites, you can also select from a list of recipes and save your favorites. When you find something you want to make, save it on your computer. Print it out when you're ready to get cooking. Recipes can also be viewed on your smartphone or tablet.

Some websites let you search for recipes based on ingredients. Simply enter a few items that you have on hand. The site will return a list of dishes you can make with those items. There are also websites that let you adjust the number of servings. Enter how many servings you need. Then the ingredients and recipe will update to show the necessary amounts.

# Chapter 4

## Following a Recipe

Most recipes begin with a list of ingredients. Before you start cooking, read this list. Make sure you have everything you need.

Get out all the ingredients. Put them on the counter. Then you can follow the recipe without stopping to look for something.

## In a Pinch: Common Ingredient Substitutions

Even the most well-organized cook can run out of an important ingredient. Use this chart to know what other ingredients you can use to replace something you don't have. Be aware that substituting ingredients might affect the taste or texture of a food.

| Ingredient | Amount | Substitution |
|---|---|---|
| baking powder | 1 teaspoon | $1/4$ teaspoon baking soda plus $1/2$ teaspoon cream of tartar plus $1/4$ teaspoon cornstarch |
| baking soda | 1 teaspoon | 3 teaspoons baking powder |
| bread crumbs | 1 cup | 1 cup cracker crumbs or 1 cup ground oats |
| broth (beef or chicken) | 1 cup | 1 bouillon cube plus 1 cup boiling water or 1 cup vegetable broth |
| brown sugar (light) | 1 cup, packed | 1 cup white sugar plus 1 tablespoon molasses |
| butter | 1 cup | 1 cup margarine or 1 cup shortening plus $1/2$ teaspoon salt |
| chocolate (semisweet) | 1 ounce | 1 ounce unsweetened baking chocolate plus 1 tablespoon sugar |
| egg | 1 whole | $1/4$ cup liquid egg substitute or half a banana mashed with $1/2$ teaspoon baking powder |
| garlic | 1 clove | $1/8$ teaspoon garlic powder |
| heavy cream | 1 cup | $3/4$ cup whole milk plus $1/4$ cup unsalted butter |
| herbs (fresh) | 1 tablespoon chopped fresh | 1 teaspoon (chopped or whole leaf) dried herbs |
| ketchup | 1 cup | 1 cup tomato sauce plus 2 tablespoons vinegar plus $1/4$ cup sugar |
| vegetable oil | 1 cup | 1 cup applesauce |
| vinegar | 1 teaspoon | 1 teaspoon lemon or lime juice or 1 teaspoon malt vinegar or 1 teaspoon apple cider vinegar |
| white sugar | 1 cup | 1 cup light brown sugar or $3/4$ cup honey or maple syrup |
| yogurt | 1 cup | 1 cup sour cream |

# Learn the Vocabulary

Cooking has a language all its own. To understand a recipe, you need to know the special vocabulary of cooking.

The following lists contain some words you're likely to see in a cookbook.

## Cutting Methods

- **Chop:** Cut the food into irregular, pea-sized pieces.

- **Finely chop:** Cut the food into pieces smaller than peas.

- **Cube:** Cut the food into ½-inch strips. Stack and line up the strips. Then cut crosswise to form cubes.

- **Dice:** Cut the food into ¼-inch strips. Stack and line up the strips. Then cut crosswise to form small pieces.

- **Grate:** Rub the food across a grater to make fine pieces.

- **Mince:** Cut the food into tiny, irregularly shaped pieces.

- **Shred:** Cut the food into thin strips by moving it over a grater or by using a knife.

- **Finely shred:** Cut the food into very thin strips by moving it over a grater or by using a knife.

- **Slice and bias-slice:** To slice, cut vertically down through food. To bias-slice, cut holding the knife at a 45-degree angle to the cutting surface.

### Spices to Keep in the Cabinet

Spices can liven up any dish and make it uniquely your own. Here are a few spices you should always have on hand:

- **Salt and black pepper:** Salt and pepper are the two most common seasonings in everyday cooking.

- **Garlic powder:** This is another popular seasoning. Garlic powder can also be used as a substitute for salt.

- **Cajun seasoning:** This is a combination of several spices. Its flavor is often described as both smoky and spicy. Cajun seasoning can be used to spice up many foods.

- **Crushed red pepper flakes:** Red pepper flakes add spicy flavor to foods. They are also believed to help increase the body's metabolism.

- **Ground cumin:** Cumin has a strong smoky flavor. Many Latin American dishes use it. It's also used in chili, barbeque sauce, and other sauces and dips.

- **Cinnamon:** Both sweet and savory foods often contain cinnamon. This spice is believed to have many health benefits.

**Cooking Methods**

- **Bake:** Cook food in the dry heat of an oven. The food may be covered or uncovered.

- **Boil:** Heat a liquid over high heat. Bubbles should rise steadily and break on the surface.

- **Broil:** Cook food a measured distance from the direct, dry heat of an oven.

- **Deep-fry:** Submerge food in very hot oil. Stir food and remove when the outer layer is golden brown and crisp.

- **Grill:** Cook food on a metal rack above a dry heat source. This may be propane gas, wood, or charcoal.

- **Panfry:** Cook food in a frying pan on a stove with a small amount of butter or oil. Use a spatula to turn the food over so it cooks evenly.

- **Poach:** Cook food partly or completely by placing it into a simmering liquid.

- **Simmer:** Heat a liquid over low heat. Bubbles should form and begin to burst below the surface.

- **Steam:** Cook food in the steam given off by boiling water. Place the food in a metal basket, a bamboo steamer, or a rack set above the water. Cover the pot and steam until the food is done.

- **Stir-fry:** Cook food quickly over high heat in a lightly oiled wok or skillet. Lift and turn the food constantly.

## Avoiding Kitchen Injuries

Many people get hurt while cooking and cleaning up. Injuries can include cuts, burns, and falls. Eye injuries and reactions to spices and chemicals are also common.

To avoid getting hurt, follow these guidelines:

- Maintain a clean and organized workspace.
- Keep your knives sharp. Store them properly.
- While using a knife, always make cuts away from your body.
- When holding the food you're cutting, curl up your fingers into your hand.
- Use utensils to move foods in and out of hot liquids. Never use your fingers.
- Don't touch your face (especially your eyes) while chopping peppers or other spicy foods.
- Keep floors clean by immediately mopping up spills.
- Don't overload electrical outlets.
- Store potholders and oven mitts near the stove and oven. That way you'll be sure to use them.
- Keep a well-stocked first aid kit in a kitchen cabinet.
- Store a fire extinguisher in an easy-to-reach place near your stove.

# Caring for Clothes

Taking care of your clothes is the best way to keep them looking good. It will also help them last a long time. Caring for your clothes is easy. Clean them **promptly** and properly. Then store them carefully in a closet or dresser. Learn how to care for your clothes. Then your favorites will always be ready to wear.

## Learning Some Hard Lessons

Doing laundry never mattered much to Justin. When he lived with his family, his parents took care of that for him. His mom had tried to teach him several times. "You'll need to know how to do this someday," she said.

Justin's dad had tried to get him to take care of his clothes too. Once a week, his dad went to the dry cleaner. There, he had his shirts cleaned and pressed. He also had his suits dry-cleaned every few weeks. Using these services was expensive. But it was necessary for taking care of his nice clothes.

None of this interested Justin though. He only cared about one thing. That was finding clean clothes in his dresser when he opened the drawers.

Now Justin wishes he'd paid attention. He's been living on his own for a few months. In that time, he's ruined a lot of clothes trying to care for them.

In fact, Justin's first load of laundry was a disaster. He'd put a new red T-shirt in with his light-colored clothing. Washing the load in hot water had been a bad idea. All his light-colored clothing turned pink. His new T-shirt had also shrunk. Now it is too small.

Justin has ruined some clothes trying to iron them too. When he tried to press a shirt, the iron was too hot. It left a burn mark on the collar.

Later, Justin tried to press a pair of dress pants. He thought this would be faster and cheaper than having them dry-cleaned. But pressing a crease down the pant leg made a dark stain. Justin realized too late that the pants were dirty. He ended up ruining them.

# Chapter 1

## Organizing a Closet and Dresser

Being kind to your clothes will keep them in good shape. This includes storing them properly in a closet or dresser.

Keeping your closet and dresser organized is key. Your clothes will stay clean and wrinkle-free. They'll be ready when you want to wear them. Organizing your clothes will also make getting dressed easy.

## Tips for Organizing Your Closet

- To keep shirts and dresses hanging straight, button their top buttons.

- Store similar clothes together. For example, keep all shirts together and all pants together.

- Don't hang knit clothes unless they're woven very tightly and you wear them often. If you do hang a knit item, fold it once the long way. Then hang it over the bar on the hanger. For extra care, put crisp white tissue paper in the fold. This prevents creasing.

- Once in a while, leave the closet door slightly open. This lets the air move around. It will keep your closet fresh.

- Hang small packets of fragrant herbs in your closet. This will keep clothes smelling good.

# Tools for Organizing Your Closet

Organizing your closet will be easier if you have the right tools. Here are a few to have on hand:

**Hangers**

- Keep extra hangers in your closet. That way, one is always available when you need it.

- Use padded hangers for knits. Try wooden hangers for coats and jackets.

- Avoid crushing your clothes by spacing hangers as far apart as possible. Using padded and wooden hangers will make this easier.

**Hanging Bags, Racks, and Shelves**

- Use hanging racks and shelves to store shoes. Doing so will make it easier to keep the floor of your closet clean. (Keeping the floor clean will discourage moths and carpet beetles. These pests can ruin clothes.)

- Use shelves for sweaters and other knit items you don't want to hang.

- Store clothes from different seasons in hanging bags. This protects them from dust.

## How to Clean Your Closet

1. To prepare, get three boxes. Label one "Trash." On another, write "Out of Place." The third will be a "Donate" box. Also buy several stackable bins.

2. Pick one section of the closet to work on. Maybe start with a shelf or the floor.

3. Take everything out of the section.

4. Look at each item. Ask yourself if you've used it in the past year. If not, put it in the "Trash" or "Donate" box.

5. Does an item belong somewhere else? Place it in the "Out of Place" box. Find the proper place for it later.

6. Sort the items you want to keep:

   • Hang clothing that belongs on hangers.

   • Put shoes and other items on shelves or racks, if possible.

   • Place the remaining items in labeled bins. You might label these "Purses" or "Softball Gear."

7. Arrange the labeled bins. Make the ones you use most often easy to reach.

8. Repeat this process with each section of your closet. You can use this method in other parts of your home too.

## Tips for Organizing Your Dresser

- Line dresser drawers with shelf paper or drawer liners. Doing so will prevent damage to the clothing from splinters or chemicals in the wood.

- Some liners smell good. But avoid sticky or prepasted paper. The glue may attract bugs.

- If possible, store clothes in many shallow drawers rather than a few deep ones. Tightly packed clothes get wrinkled. They're also harder to find.

- If you have to stack clothes in drawers, put lighter items on top of heavier items.

- Put knits and clothes made of soft fabrics in the dresser, not the closet. Hanging them will make them lose their shape.

- Before putting an item of clothing in a drawer, press it out flat. Then either roll or fold the item neatly.

- When folding clothes, put folds where they won't show when the clothes are worn. For example, fold along seams or the waistband.

### Problems With Scented Products

Scented air fresheners, shelf papers, and other products may make your closet or dresser smell good. But over time, they can cause health problems. The scents get into your clothes. Then you carry them to work or school.

Some people develop serious reactions to the chemicals in these products. Symptoms include a runny nose, watery eyes, and headaches. People may also have trouble breathing or become nauseous, dizzy, or tired.

Because of health issues with scents, some workplaces have a no-fragrance policy.

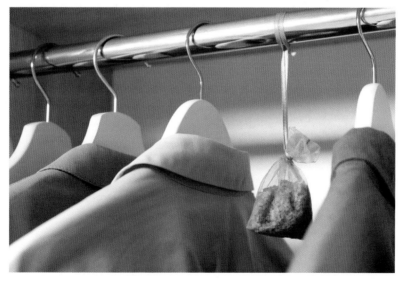

# Chapter 2

## Doing the Laundry

How you care for your clothes is important. Clothes last longer when they're well taken care of.

Taking care of your clothes is also important to your appearance. After all, your clothing makes a statement about you.

For both these reasons, you need to learn how to do laundry correctly.

## Follow the Rules

Doing laundry isn't hard. Following three simple rules will keep your whites white and your colors bright.

### Rule 1: Sort your laundry before you load it into the washing machine.

- Wash similar-colored clothes together. Make sure everything is of the same darkness or brightness. In other words, wash lights in one load, brights in another, and darks in a third load.

- Wash whites only with other whites. Clothing must have no color at all. Other colors can fade or bleed onto your whites. This means a sock with a red stripe does not go in with the whites.

- Also sort clothes according to how dirty they are. Wash very dirty clothes in their own load. Before washing extremely dirty clothes, soak them in soapy water and then rinse them.

**Rule 2: Deal with stains before you do the laundry.**

Washing something in hot water can make it impossible to remove a stain. Drying in a hot dryer can too. This is because heat sets stains. It makes them **permanent**.

For best results, treat stains as soon as possible. Fresh stains are easier to remove than old stains.

Here are a few more tips:

- Use a stain remover. These are sold in stores. You can also make your own. Mix powdered laundry detergent with a little water to make a paste. Rub this into the stain. Rubbing a little liquid detergent into the stain works too.

- Lightly scrub the stain using a small brush. A fingernail brush or an old toothbrush will work. Then wash the clothing as usual.

## Tips for Treating Stains

### General Stain Treatment

- Dab at the stain using a wet sponge. Use lukewarm water.
- For whites, follow up with bleach if necessary.
- Don't dry the item in the dryer until the stain has been completely removed.

### Specific Types of Stains

- **Fruit, wine, juice, rust, or tea:** Stretch the fabric over a bowl or sink. Then pour boiling water through the stain.
- **Blood:** Mix one part hydrogen peroxide, one part baking soda, and two parts water. Apply mix to the stain. Let sit for 20 minutes. Wash as usual.
- **Ink:** Rub hairspray into the stain. Rinse with cold water.

- **Chocolate:** Rub stain with dish soap. Rinse with cold water.
- **Coffee:** Dab the stain with rubbing alcohol. Rinse with cold water.
- **Grass:** Make a paste with white vinegar and baking soda. Rub paste into stain. Let sit for 15 minutes, then rinse.
- **Grease, oil, or lipstick:** Rub with cornstarch or baking soda. Let sit for 20 minutes. Brush off, then wash as usual.
- **Sweat:** Make a paste with baking soda and water. Rub paste into stain. Wash in hot water.

## Rule 3: Use the proper heat settings.

Using the wrong water temperature can ruin your clothing. Clothes might shrink, colors may bleed, and white items can turn gray. Check the labels inside your clothes for more information.

### Guidelines for Heat Settings

- **Whites:** Hot water wash, cold rinse

- **Wash-and-wear colored fabrics:** Warm water wash, cold rinse

- **Elastic fabrics:** Cold water wash, cold rinse

- **Synthetic fabrics:** Warm water wash, cold rinse

- **Colored fabrics that bleed:** Cold water wash, cold rinse

- **Woolens:** Cold water wash, cold rinse

## Tips for Clothing Care

- Wash clothes only when they're dirty. If clothes are wrinkled but not dirty, iron them.

- Iron clothes only when they're wrinkled. But *don't* iron dirty clothes. This can set stains.

- Air-dry clothes as much as possible. Hang them or lay them flat.

- Follow the care instructions on clothing labels.

- Fix rips, tears, and loose buttons as soon as possible. Don't wash clothes until after they've been mended.

- Treat stains as soon as possible with stain remover. Then wash the stained item immediately in cold water. Repeat if necessary.

# Chapter 3

## Information on Clothing Labels

Some clothes should be washed only in cold water. Others should be washed in warm or hot water. Rinsing in cold water is fine for nearly all kinds of clothes. Plus, using cold water saves energy.

How do you know if you're using the right temperatures for your clothes? Check the care labels. These may be small fabric tags that are sewn into clothing. They might also be printed on the inside of the fabric. Look for them near the collar, waistband, or side seams.

# Labeling Requirements

By law in the United States, all clothing must have care labels. The only exceptions are hats, gloves, and most shoes.

Care labels must:

- tell what types of **fibers** the **garment** is made from.

- note what country the garment was made in.

- list washing or dry-cleaning instructions.

- be easy to read.

- be permanent for the life of the garment.

- warn if a garment can't be cleaned by a certain method.

- list the appropriate water temperature, if certain temperatures will harm the item.

- note the appropriate dryer setting, if hot air will harm the item.

- tell the recommended iron setting, if certain settings will harm the item.

- mention that bleach is not safe or that only non-chlorine bleach is safe.

## Reading the Label

Here is an example of what a care label looks like:

Learn the meanings of common laundry symbols. Then you'll understand what the label is telling you to do. You may also see the wash symbol with a temperature inside. This is how hot or cold the water should be. It may also have one or more dots. The dryer and iron symbols may have one or more dots as well. More dots means that a higher heat setting can be used. You can also find clothing care information online.

# Common Laundry Symbols

| Symbol | Variations | | | | Warnings |
|---|---|---|---|---|---|

Wash

 Normal     Permanent Press     Delicate     Hand Wash     Do Not Wash

Bleach

 Any Bleach    Non-Chlorine Bleach Only     Do Not Bleach

 Normal     Permanent Press     Delicate     Do Not Dry     Dry in Shade

Dry

 Hang to Dry     Drip Dry     Dry Flat      Do Not Wring

Iron

 High Heat     Medium Heat     Low Heat     No Steam

Dry Clean

 Short Cycle     Reduced Moisture     Low Heat     No Steam

 Any Solvent     Do Not Dry Clean

(A) Any Solvent    (P) Any Solvent Except Trichloroethylene    (F) Petroleum Solvent Only

## Clothing Label Requirements

Clothing labels are overseen by the Federal Trade Commission (FTC). This is part of the U.S. government. The FTC works with clothing manufacturers to provide two kinds of clothing labels.

1. **Care labels:** These provide instructions for washing and drying. They also note anything that could harm an item, such as ironing or machine washing.

2. **Content labels:** These say what the fabric is made of. They also note the country it came from. The company that made the product or brought it to the United States is also indicated.

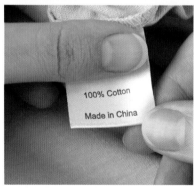

## How to Dry Clothes Flat

Care labels that specify air-drying also sometimes say to "dry flat." Doing so prevents the extra water weight from stretching knitted garments, such as sweaters.

To dry a clothing item flat, follow these steps:

1. **Prepare a space.** One way is to lay a towel on a table. Another is to use a flat drying rack.

2. **Place the garment.** Lay the item on the towel or rack. Carefully arrange it in its proper shape. Check pockets, collars, and necklines.

3. **Let it dry.** Drying can take a day or more. It depends on how thick the fabric is. When the top of the item is dry, turn it over. This will speed up drying.

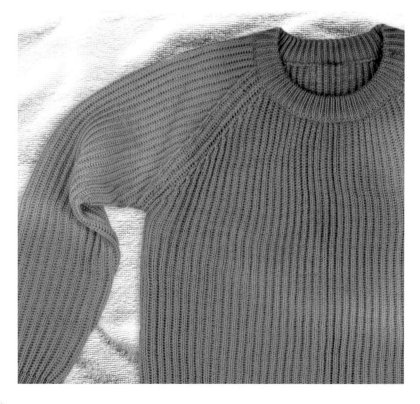

# Chapter 4

## Ironing, Dry Cleaning, and Storing Clothes

Some of the clothes you purchase will be for work or special occasions. These clothes may require extra care. Your employer might expect your shirts and slacks to be ironed. Some suits and dresses may need to be dry cleaned. Clothes for certain seasons will last longer if they are stored properly when not in use.

### Tips for Ironing

- Most fabrics are easier to iron if they are **damp**. Take clothes out of the dryer before they're completely dry. You can also mist dry clothes with a spray bottle. A steam iron can be used to dampen clothes as you iron.

- Use **starch** to dampen **tailored** shirts and other items you want to look crisp. Spray the starch lightly and evenly across the item. You can buy spray starch or make your own. Mix one tablespoon of cornstarch into two cups of water. Pour the mixture into a spray bottle.

- Check the heat setting on the iron. Choose the setting that's appropriate for the fabric. If the setting is too hot, you could ruin your clothes.

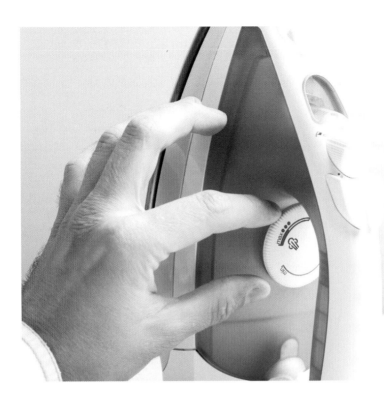

**Ironing Tips**

- Check the iron setting. Make sure it's correct before touching the iron to the clothing.

- Iron those items with "High" heat settings first. Then each time you lower the setting, give the iron a minute or two to cool down.

- Iron collars, cuffs, and hems on the inside first. This prevents puckering. Then turn over and iron on the outside.

- Put a rolled-up towel inside a sleeve or pant leg to prevent creases.

- Iron wash-and-wear fabrics inside out to avoid making them shiny. You can also cover them with a cotton dish towel or pillowcase before ironing on the outside.

- Avoid creating new wrinkles by moving freshly ironed sections away from you.

## Tips for Dry Cleaning

- Dry-clean clothes as infrequently as possible. Why? The dry-cleaning process is hard on them. Clothing that's only wrinkled may not need dry cleaning. If you ask, most cleaners will press a garment without cleaning it. This is easier on your clothes. It costs less too.

- Don't have something pressed that's even slightly dirty. The heat involved may make a nearly invisible stain turn brown. It could also set the stain permanently.

- The dry-cleaning process can cause slight color changes in clothing. Always dry-clean both parts of a two-piece outfit at the same time. This is true even if only one piece needs cleaning. Otherwise, you might end up with a suit jacket that's lighter than the pants or skirt.

## How Does Dry Cleaning Work?

1. **Tagging and pretreating:** Each garment is inspected, and its care needs are tagged to it. Then any stains are pretreated.

2. **Washing:** Clothes are put in a special machine. This is like a large washing machine. A liquid chemical called perchloroethylene, or perc, is pumped through the machine as it spins. The process is called "dry cleaning" because no water is used.

3. **Rinsing:** A drain cycle spins the clothes to remove the perc.

4. **Drying:** Warm air blows through the machine.

5. **Inspection:** The person operating the machine looks for any remaining spots and treats them.

6. **Pressing:** A pressing machine uses steam and pressure to straighten the garments. Then it vacuums out the steam, leaving the clothes dry. Some companies press garments by hand.

7. **Bagging:** Tags are removed. Garments are placed in bags and hung up. They are now ready to be picked up.

## Tips for Storing Clothes

- Never store dirty clothes. Over time, dirt and stains become much harder to remove. Some types of stains may also attract bugs.

- Before storing clothes, make sure all traces of detergent have been removed. Even tiny traces can cause chemical changes over time.

- Don't store items that have been starched. Starch attracts bugs called silverfish.

- Store seasonal clothes in clean plastic bins or boxes. A clean suitcase works too. You can also use empty drawers in an extra dresser. Place hanging clothes in a hanging bag and store them in a closet.

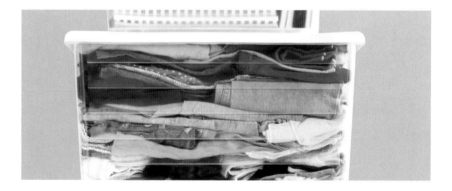

- Covering clothes will help keep out water, dust, mold, bacteria, and smoke. Use **muslin** bags or cover clothing with sheets. Avoid using plastic bags for some clothes or for long periods of time. These cut off air. Without air, leather and suede will dry out. Other fabrics will slowly break down. Moisture trapped in plastic bags can form mildew and leave stains.

# Home Maintenance and Decorating

Wouldn't it be nice to have a live-in cleaning person? Your home would always be spotless. What if you hired an interior designer? Every room would be decorated exactly how you wanted. These services can be expensive. Not everyone can afford them. It's important to know how to clean and decorate your home yourself. This won't always be easy. But you'll feel satisfied knowing that you did it yourself.

# Fixing Up a Fixer-Upper

Nikki had heard people talk about "fixer-uppers." She now knew what that term meant. Her family had just moved to a small town. They'd bought a house that was almost 100 years old. It was exactly the kind of home her parents had always dreamed of owning.

The house needed a lot of work. First, it needed a thorough cleaning. The previous owners hadn't done much housekeeping. Everything in the house was dusty.

Scrubbing the wood and tile floors got them sparkling clean. But shampooing the carpet did little good. It would have to be torn up and replaced. Not cleaning the carpet for so many years had ruined it.

The kitchen was especially dirty. Cleaning thick grease off the oven and stove required some heavy-duty cleaning products. Nikki and her sister worked a whole day to get the kitchen clean.

Next came the bedrooms. Nikki was excited to start decorating hers. First, she repaired some small holes in the walls. Later, she was going to paint the room. She'd already picked out the type and color of paint.

Nikki decided to keep her old bedroom furniture. She had a bed, a dresser, and a desk. There was also a big, heavy mirror. This wouldn't be easy to hang. Her dad would help her make sure it was mounted securely.

Finally, it was time to decorate. Nikki had some inexpensive ideas. She'd read about finding cool artwork, flower pots, and other items on local resale apps. Who knew what treasures Nikki would find?

# Chapter 1

## Following a Cleaning Schedule

Eli, Chen, and Justin are roommates. The house they share has three bedrooms and one bathroom. They have two cats.

When the roommates moved in together, they sat down to talk. Eli, Chen, and Justin all agreed. They'd rather have a clean house than a messy one. But the more they talked, they realized they had two questions.

## Basic Cleaning Equipment and Supplies

### Cleaning Equipment

- vacuum
- broom and dustpan
- mop and bucket
- toilet brush and caddy
- toilet plunger
- squeegee (for windows and shower)
- dust cloths and feather duster
- rags and soft cloths
- sponges
- scrub brush
- rubber gloves

### Cleaning Supplies

- all-purpose cleaner
- disinfectant cleaner
- window cleaner
- abrasive cleaner
- household ammonia
- dishwasher detergent
- dish soap
- white vinegar
- baking soda
- chlorine bleach
- spot carpet cleaner
- laundry detergent

## What Needs to Be Done?

None of the roommates had ever had their own place before. All three had lived at home with their families. They'd helped out. But they hadn't been **responsible** for cleaning an entire house.

The roommates decided to make a list of jobs. They started with one they knew about. This was cleaning their bedrooms. Then they wrote down some other jobs they'd done in the past. These were cleaning the bathroom, emptying the garbage, and taking care of pets.

Eli, Chen, and Justin split some jobs into several parts. For instance, some of the kitchen jobs needed to be done on an ongoing basis. They decided that each roommate should clean up his own mess after using the kitchen. Other jobs needed to be done less often—like mopping the floor.

With some help from parents and friends, the roommates came up with a list of jobs. That led to their second question.

## Housecleaning Tips for Pet Owners

- Use a lint brush to remove pet hair from furniture.

- Vacuum floors every few days to pick up pet hair. You can also sweep and then wipe the floor with a damp mop.

- Place a large doormat near the door that pets use. This will collect the dirt they track in. Shake out the mat every couple of days.

- Bathe and groom pets regularly. This can help reduce shedding and odors.

- Provide pets with a towel, rug, blanket, or bed to lie on. Launder the item regularly. Add vinegar to the wash water to get rid of odors.

- Clean out litter boxes daily. Replace the litter weekly.

- Small pets might live in a cage or tank. Clean out the cage or tank weekly. Replace all bedding with fresh material. This will prevent odors.

- Clean up pet accidents immediately. Pick up as much material as possible. Soak up wetness with a paper towel. Spray the area with an enzyme cleaner. Then blot using a clean, damp rag. Using this special kind of cleaner will help get rid of waste odors.

## Who's Going to Do the Work?

Of course, no one wanted to be responsible for doing all the work.
Eli, Chen, and Justin made a schedule of jobs that would need to
be done regularly.

They decided that the schedule would be in effect for one week.
After a week, the roommates would rotate the jobs assigned to
each person. The week after that, they would rotate the jobs again.

## Creating a Cleaning Schedule

Setting up a cleaning schedule can be very helpful. You and the people you live with will have an easier time keeping your home tidy. There are many ways to make a plan. Find apps on your phone or tablet. Some turn cleaning into a game. This makes chores fun. Another option is to create a cleaning schedule on the computer. A spreadsheet program can help. Everyone in your house should have access to the file. You can also print out a copy each week and hang it up for all to see. Dry-erase boards make it easy to split up cleaning tasks. But schedules don't need to be fancy or complicated. Using just a pen and paper works well too.

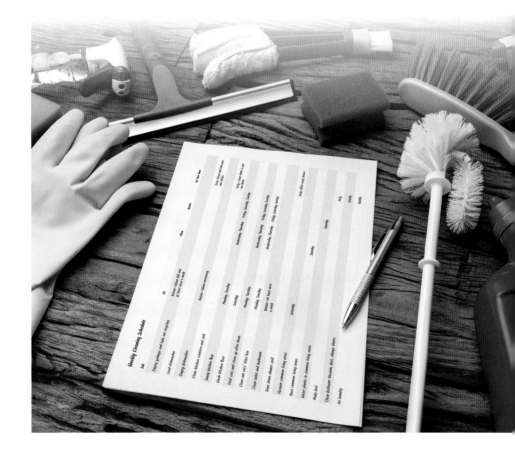

## Weekly Cleaning Schedule

| Job | Eli |
|---|---|
| Empty garbage and take out recycling | Rotate—When full, but at least once a week |
| Load dishwasher | |
| Empty dishwasher | Rotate—When necessary |
| Clean kitchen counters and sink | |
| Sweep kitchen floor | Monday, Tuesday |
| Wash kitchen floor | Saturday |
| Feed cats and clean up after them | Monday, Tuesday |
| Clean out cats' litter box | Monday, Tuesday |
| Clean toilet and bathroom | Rotate—At least once a week |
| Wipe down shower stall | |
| Vacuum common living areas | Saturday |
| Dust common living areas | |
| Water plants in common living areas | |
| Make bed | |
| Clean bedroom: Vacuum, dust, change sheets | |
| Do laundry | |

| Chen | Justin | Do Your Own |
|---|---|---|
| | | Daily—Rinse and load your own dishes |
| | | Daily—Clean them as you use them |
| Wednesday, Thursday | Friday, Saturday, Sunday | |
| Wednesday, Thursday | Friday, Saturday, Sunday | |
| Wednesday, Thursday | Friday, Saturday, Sunday | |
| | | Daily—After every shower |
| Saturday | | |
| | Saturday | |
| | | Daily |
| | | Weekly |
| | | Weekly |

# Chapter 2

## Understanding Directions on Cleaning Products

Ty spilled a glass of juice on the carpet. Right away, he soaked it up with paper towels. Then he poured a little laundry detergent on the area. He rubbed it with a wet dish towel.

Had Ty cleaned the carpet properly? He thought so. But the next day, he realized the juice had left a red spot. Now what could he do?

## Read the Instructions Before You Clean

Ty didn't want to hire a professional service to clean the whole living room. After all, the rest of the carpet was clean. All he wanted was to remove the spot.

He bought a product intended to remove stains from carpets. Before Ty began to clean the spot, he read the product label. This was on the back of the bottle:

# FORMULA 208
## CARPET SPOT CLEANER
### Cleans a Variety of Tough Stains!

Formula 208 Carpet Cleaner is safe yet powerful. It's effective on a variety of tough spots and stains, including tracked-in dirt, grease, and food spills. It even cleans up the worst messes, such as pet stains, spaghetti sauce, grape/berry juice, and mud from foot traffic. Formula 208 Carpet Cleaner has special ingredients to resist dirt and stains too. This makes it easier to clean the same area next time.

**Fabric Safety:** Use only on wool, nylon, and other synthetic carpets. Safe to use on stain-resistant carpets.

**Before Cleaning:** Test a hidden area of carpet to make sure it's *colorfast*. Remove loose dirt from the area that needs spot cleaning. For wet spills, blot the area with a clean, absorbent cloth. Then follow the directions below.

**Directions:** Spray soiled area with Formula 208 Carpet Cleaner. Allow to sit for 3 minutes. Gently blot the area with a clean, absorbent cloth or colorfast sponge. Repeat as needed. Allow carpet to dry completely. Then vacuum. For best results, use product promptly after the spot occurs. Do not over wet carpet. Some stains will cause permanent damage even after cleaning.

**For Larger Areas:** Formula 208 Carpet Cleaner lifts out a variety of tough spots and stains. It's also good for cleaning the entire carpet.

**CAUTION:** Eye *irritant*. Avoid eye contact and *prolonged* skin contact.

**FIRST AID:** Eyes—Flush with water for 15 minutes. Skin—Rinse with water.

**IF SWALLOWED:** Drink a glass of water. Call a doctor.

**KEEP OUT OF REACH OF CHILDREN.**

## Tips for Carpet Care

- Vacuum often. Keep carpets clean. Sand and dirt cut the fibers in carpet. That makes it harder to remove dirt and stains.

- Catch dirt with doormats. Place doormats on both sides of entrances. Put one inside your home. Place another outside.

- Remove shoes at the door. Having a "no shoes" policy helps keep carpets clean. It also stops harmful substances from being tracked through your home.

- Clean stains immediately. Use a spot cleaner made for carpets. Work from the outer edges of the stain toward the center. Repeat until you can't remove any more. Then thoroughly rinse the area. Dry it quickly.

- Use a wet-dry vacuum. This will clean stains better. Several rounds of washing and rinsing often are needed.

- Vacuum before deep-cleaning the carpet. This removes dirt and sand. If you're cleaning the carpet yourself, get the water as hot as possible. Speed up the drying time with fans.

## Selecting a Vacuum

A vacuum is a big purchase. Prices range from around $50 to more than $1,000. Before you buy, check out the three main types of vacuums: upright, canister, and robotic. Know what each kind can and can't do. Also think about what features are important to you.

| | Upright | Canister | Robotic |
|---|---|---|---|
| How you use it | • Push it in front of you | • Pull it behind you | • Program schedule and let it run |
| Good qualities | • Good for pet fur<br>• Good for large spaces | • Multipurpose: cleans stairs, upholstery, and hard-to-reach areas | • Good for people with limited mobility<br>• Can set a cleaning schedule<br>• Will return to charging station on its own<br>• Some empty their own dustbins |
| Bad qualities | • Can't get into tight spaces | • Not very effective for carpet | • Can be expensive<br>• Obstacles need to be cleared from path<br>• May get stuck<br>• May need to be emptied frequently<br>• Won't work on stairs |
| Options | • May come with attachments for cleaning upholstery and hard-to-reach areas<br>• May adjust for cleaning bare floors<br>• May use a HEPA (high-efficiency particulate air) filter—good for people with allergies | • May come with attachments for different cleaning purposes<br>• May use a HEPA filter—good for people with allergies | • May come with app controls or voice command<br>• May use a HEPA filter—good for people with allergies |

## Selecting Carpet

When picking out new carpet, choosing a color often comes to mind first. But there is more to it than that. There are several kinds of carpets. They are made with different types of fibers. The type of carpet you buy will affect how much it costs. It will also affect how easy the carpet is to care for and how long it will last.

| Fiber | Positive Qualities | Negative Qualities |
|---|---|---|
| Nylon | • Very strong—wears well<br>• Fibers resist crushing<br>• Dries quickly<br>• Resists mildew<br>• Cleans easily<br>• Inexpensive | • Bleaches and fades easily<br>• Changes color from pet stains |
| Polyester | • Resists bleaching, fading, and soiling<br>• Dries quickly<br>• Some types resist stains | • Difficult to remove oily stains<br>• Fibers get tangled and matted |
| Olefin | • Resists stains<br>• Resists fading<br>• Very strong—wears well<br>• Cleans easily—bleach and chemical safe | • Fibers crush and mat easily<br>• Melts easily<br>• Friction leaves burn marks<br>• Difficult to remove oily stains<br>• Shows dirt easily |
| Wool | • Doesn't show dirt<br>• Very strong—wears well<br>• Cleans well<br>• Resists fire | • Expensive<br>• Stains easily<br>• Sensitive to chemicals<br>• Dissolves in bleach<br>• Fibers fuzz and streak easily |

# Caring for Your Floors

Not all homes have carpet. Some have wood, tile, or linoleum flooring. Keeping these areas clean is easy with the right tools. Use a broom to sweep up dirt and pet hair. You can also use a dry mop or a similar tool with a disposable pad. These pick up and trap dirt, dust, and hair.

Mop floors regularly with water and a mild cleaning solution to keep them clean and shiny. Just be sure to sweep or vacuum up any debris first. To deep clean your floors, use a steam mop.

# Chapter 3

## Easy Decorating With Pictures and Plants

Decorating can be fun. You can find ideas in magazines and catalogs. Websites and TV shows also offer inspiration.

Unfortunately, decorating can be expensive. After moving into a new home, you may not have much money left over for decorating.

Get creative. Look for easy, inexpensive ways to decorate. Start by hanging pictures. Add houseplants too.

## Where to Find Affordable Art

- Look for artwork at garage sales and estate sales. Also look at secondhand stores. While looking for artwork, keep an eye out for inexpensive frames.

- Visit a college or university with an art department. Art students often sell their work at shows or when they need money.

- Check online auction websites.

- There are many websites where artists sell their work. Designs can be printed in many sizes. They can also be printed on blankets, pillows, and more.

- Some websites offer the option of printing photos at large sizes. Have your own photos printed and hang them as wall art. You may also be able to choose from a selection of other people's photos.

## Tips for Hanging Pictures

- Hang paintings out of direct sunlight and away from drafts and dampness.

- Don't hang pictures on walls with new **drywall** or paint. This could damage the pictures.

- Avoid hanging pictures above radiators or other heaters. Don't hang pictures on parts of walls with hot pipes or chimney pipes inside. The heat will damage the pictures.

- If you want to light up artwork, use a low-voltage spotlight. Otherwise, keep artwork away from direct sources of electric light. The heat can cause damage.

- For heavy pictures, drive the picture-hanging nail into a **stud**.

- If you want to hang the picture where there is no stud, use a molly bolt. This type of bolt spreads out inside the wall. That gives the picture more support.

- A very heavy frame may need support at the bottom. You can hang a heavy picture so the bottom rests on a piece of furniture. Or you can rest the frame on a **ledge** you've attached to the wall. Small blocks of wood will also work.

# Tips for Taking Care of Houseplants

- All plants need light. But not all plants need the same amount. Find out what's good for each kind of plant you have. Then place each one closer to or farther from a window, according to its needs.

- Plants also need water. But again, they may need different amounts. Some plants need to have damp soil at all times. Others need the soil to dry out between waterings. Look up each plant's watering needs, and water it accordingly.

- Some plants need regular misting. They may need their leaves dampened daily. For these plants, buy a spray bottle and keep it handy. Don't mist plants near furniture that might be damaged by water. Take plants to the kitchen sink or outdoors, if needed.

- Plants don't like to be dusty. Use a clean cloth to gently dust their leaves. A soft brush will also work.

- Regularly remove dead leaves and flowers from plants. Doing so keeps them healthy. It makes them look better too.

- Put plants that get too big into new pots. Roots may start growing out of the bottom of the pot. This means the plant needs more room to grow. Find a bigger pot to put it in.

- Feed plants regularly. Get a good houseplant food. Follow the directions on the label. Some food can be added to the water used for watering. Other plant foods are added right to the soil.

## Easy-to-Grow Houseplants

| Type | Light Needs | Water Needs | Main Features | Safe for Pets? |
|------|-------------|-------------|---------------|----------------|
| Snake plant | Low to bright | Water when soil is dry | Cleans the air Hard to kill | Mildly toxic |
| Air plant | Bright, indirect | Mist once a week | No soil needed | Yes |
| Chinese money plant | Low | Once a week | Thick, round leaves | Yes |
| Pothos | Low to bright | Water when soil is dry | Grows quickly Long, leafy vines | No, toxic if chewed |
| Spider plant | Bright, indirect | Once a week | Produces baby plants that can be removed and potted | Yes |
| ZZ plant | Low to bright | Every one to two weeks | Cleans the air | No, toxic if chewed |
| Chinese evergreen | Low to medium | Every one to two weeks | Great plant for beginners | No, toxic if chewed |

# Chapter 4

## Repairing Walls, Paint, and Wallpaper

Even if you're careful, the walls of your home will get damaged with daily use. Luckily, many small signs of wear and tear are easily fixed.

# Repairing Wall Damage

Small nail holes and gouges
in drywall can usually be filled.
Look for an all-in-one nail-hole
patch product or a joint
compound. Use a putty knife
to fill the hole. Then allow the
repair to dry. Finally, smooth
the area with a medium- to
fine-grit sandpaper.

For larger holes, you may need to purchase a drywall repair kit. Your
local hardware store will have one. Before using the kit, remove any
loose material around the edge of the hole. Then apply the patch,
following the instructions.

## Basic Paint Safety

Painting a room can be fun, especially when you get to pick out the color and
finish. But many paints have harmful chemicals. It's not good to breathe these in.
To stay safe, make sure you open windows. Using fans can help too. Try to let a
room air out for a few days after painting before you start using it. In many places,
you can't throw paint cans in the trash. You'll need to find a special drop-off center
to take them to. This is because paint is considered hazardous waste.

# Touching Up Painted Walls

Some wall repairs will require paint touch-ups. For a stain or **scuff**, first try washing the damaged area. Use a sponge or clean rag and plain water, a mild dish soap, or a wall-cleaning solution.

If you need to paint over the area, follow these guidelines:

- Find the original paint, if possible. If it's not available, find the closest possible color and finish.

- **Prime** the wall with flat latex paint before finishing with a shiny paint. (Flat paint colors are self-priming.) Use sealer to cover stains such as ink and grease.

- Make sure the paint is mixed well. Shake the can or stir the paint just before using it.

- For a small touch-up, use a brush. On a larger area, use a small roller.

- Before painting the whole area, try a small test patch first. Let the paint dry. Then see how it looks before finishing the job.

- "Feather" the edges into the surrounding area with a nearly dry brush or roller. To do so, move out from the center with several light strokes. Lift the brush or roller off the surface as you go. With a brush, you can also try to dab the edges of the touch-up. This will help them blend in.

- There might be an obvious difference between the original finish and your touch-ups. In this case, you may need to repaint the whole wall.

### Getting Ready to Paint

- Take everything out of the room. If there are items you can't move out, push them to the center of the room. Cover them with a sheet to keep paint off.

- Cover the floor with a drop cloth. This will catch any spills or drips.

- Fill in any holes and cracks with putty. When dry, use sandpaper to smooth the surfaces.

- Wash walls to remove dust, dirt, and grease.

- Paint over any stains with a special sealant. This will stop them from showing through the paint.

- Use painter's tape to mask (seal off) edges around windows and doorways. You can also mask edges along the floor and ceiling. This prevents paint from getting into areas you aren't painting.

- Remove switch plates and outlet plates.

- Change into clothing that you don't mind getting paint on.

## How to Choose Paint

1. **Select the color.** Painting a wall is easiest if you choose a color that's similar to that of the ceiling and trim. Using a contrasting color requires greater skill and care to paint straight lines along the edges. Also, fewer coats of paint are needed to cover an old color if the new color is similar to it.

2. **Decide on oil or latex (water-based) paint.** Latex is easy to use, dries quickly, and doesn't have a strong smell. Also, brushes and other painting tools can be cleaned up using water. Oil-based paint is more durable and washable. It's good for molding and trim. Painting tools must be cleaned using special chemicals when using oil-based paints.

3. **Specify interior or exterior paint.** The two kinds of paint are designed for different uses. Interior paints dry harder and are available in more finishes. They're also more washable than exterior paints. Exterior paints are designed to last in all kinds of weather. Also, the chemicals that make them weather resistant may make them unsafe for indoor use.

4. **Pick the finish.** "Finish" is the amount of shine or gleam a paint has. Types of finishes range from a soft look with no sheen to a hard look that's shiny and reflective.

## Selecting a Paint Finish

| Finish Type | Features | Uses |
| --- | --- | --- |
| Flat or matte | • No sheen<br>• Hides wall damage<br>• Least washable<br>• Needs only one or two coats<br>• Easy to touch up | • Ceilings<br>• Living rooms<br>• Bedrooms<br>• Damaged walls<br>• Garages |
| Eggshell or satin | • Soft, warm sheen<br>• More washable and stain-resistant than flat<br>• Covers imperfections | • Bedrooms<br>• Hallways<br>• Family rooms<br>• Living rooms<br>• Bathrooms<br>• Kitchens<br>• Dining Rooms<br>• Laundry rooms |
| Semi-gloss | • More sheen<br>• More resistant to dirt and scuff marks<br>• Washable | • Kitchens<br>• Bathrooms<br>• Trim<br>• Doors<br>• Windows<br>• Cabinets |
| Gloss or high-gloss | • Shiniest, most reflective sheen<br>• Highlights wall damage<br>• Most washable and stain resistant<br>• Requires the most coats of paint<br>• Easiest to clean | • Trim<br>• Doors<br>• Woodwork |

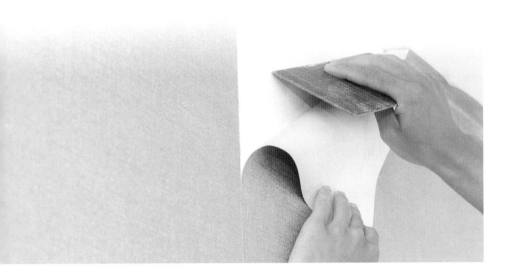

## Repairing Loose Wallpaper Edges and Tears

As wallpaper ages, the edges sometimes loosen or tear. This problem is seen more in older homes.

You don't have to replace the wallpaper. Instead, use this simple method of repair:

1. For a loose edge, use a wet sponge to dampen the damaged area.

2. Carefully lift the wallpaper away from the wall.

3. Apply a thin, even layer of wallpaper **adhesive** to the back of the wallpaper.

4. Press the wallpaper back in place. Sponge off any extra adhesive.

Avoid soaking the wallpaper, or the adhesive behind it could become loose.

## Making Your House a Home

Getting your own place is an exciting life event. It can also be a little scary. This may be the first time you'll be grocery shopping and cooking for yourself. Perhaps doing laundry is new to you. Maybe you've never had to clean much before. Then there is painting and decorating. You'll need time and money to get things done. Luckily, living independently without breaking the bank isn't hard. Learn how to tackle everyday household tasks. Then you'll be able to make your house a home.

# GLOSSARY

**adhesive:** a substance used to make things stick together

**agriculture:** the job or science of farming

**aisle:** a narrow space where people walk

**bargain:** something bought or sold for a price that is lower than the actual value

**batch:** an amount of something made all at one time

**bulk:** something made in large amounts or in large containers

**comparison shop:** to look at two or more similar items while shopping to see which is better or has the lowest price

**condiment:** a sauce or flavoring added to food to give it more flavor

**coupon:** part of an advertisement that offers savings on an item or service; can be paper or digital

**dab:** to gently touch something with fast, small motions

**damp:** slightly wet

**drywall:** large sheets of plaster covered with thick paper that are used to build walls and ceilings

**expiration date:** the date when a food item should no longer be sold because its quality won't be as good

**fiber:** a thin thread of material used to make cloth; also a plant material in some foods that helps with digestion

**gadget:** a small, helpful device

**garment:** an article of clothing

**gouge:** a deep hole or cut

**habit:** an action that a person repeats regularly

**ingredient:** a food or spice that is combined with other foods and spices to make a recipe

**ledge:** a narrow raised surface on a wall

**logical:** in a way that makes sense

**muslin:** a thin, loosely woven cotton cloth

**nutritious:** containing substances that people need to grow properly and be healthy

**pantry:** a small room where food is kept

**permanent:** lasting a very long time or forever

**pest:** an unwanted or harmful creature

**prime:** to cover a surface with special paint so it's ready for the final layer of paint

**produce:** fresh vegetables and fruits

**promptly:** without delay

**ready-made:** prepared in advance and packaged so that the food or item can be eaten or used immediately

**recipe:** step-by-step directions to make a food or drink

**responsible:** having the duty of taking care of something

**scuff:** a mark that is made by scraping something

**seasonal:** occurring or used during a certain time of the year

**staple:** a food item used in many different meals and recipes

**starch:** a liquid or powder used to make clothing stiff

**stud:** an upright piece of wood used to build the frame of a wall

**tailored:** made or changed to meet a specific purpose or need

**unit price:** the cost of a single thing that is a part of a larger group; found by dividing the cost by the quantity

**utensil:** a simple device, such as a fork or spatula, used for doing kitchen tasks

# LIFE SKILLS HANDBOOKS

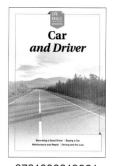

**Car and Driver**

9781680219821

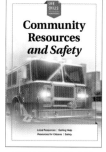

**Community Resources and Safety**

9781680219913

**Consumer Spending**

9781680219838

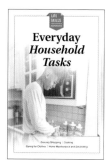

**Everyday Household Tasks**

9781680219845

**Getting Ahead at Work**

9781680219852

**Health and Wellness**

9781680219869

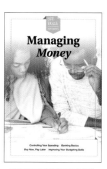

**Managing Money**

9781680219883

**Moving Out on Your Own**

9781680219890

**Transportation**

9781680219906

**Workplace Readiness**

9781680219876

## For more information, visit:
www.sdlback.com/life-skills-handbooks